College. Livingstone

The Living Stone

Vol. II

College. Livingstone

The Living Stone
Vol. II

ISBN/EAN: 9783744677295

Printed in Europe, USA, Canada, Australia, Japan

Cover: Foto ©Suzi / pixelio.de

More available books at **www.hansebooks.com**

THE
LIVING-STONE,

PUBLISHED MONTHLY.

In the Interest of the cause which Livingstone College
Represents, and for the benefit of Students, Alumni.

Vol II.   Salisbury, N. C., October, '90.   No. 3.

CONTENTS:

——:o:——

GEO. H. WILKERSON, '93--------------------------EDITOR.
W. F. FONVIELLE, '94------------------------MANAGING EDITOR.

SUBSORIPTION PRICE F.FTY CENTS PER YEAR IN ADVANCE·

Entered as Second-Class Matter at the Post-Office at Salisbury, N. C.

Single Copies 10 Cents.

THE

LIVING-STONE.

| VOL. II. | OCTOBER, 1890. | NO. 3. |

THE TREAD OF THE Y. M. C. A. IN THE SOUTH.

A PAPEL READ AT THE ANNIVERSARY OF THE Y. M. C. A. OF LIVING-
STONE COLLEGE. BY W. H. DAVENPORT.

We have studied the tread of monarchs, we have studied the advance of civilization, we have observed the movements of, art, we have
marvelled at the universal advance of Christianity ; but we divert your
attention from the triumphs of heroes, the conquests of Kings, the acquisitions of science in order that your interest in the movement of the Y.
M. C. A. may be the more intensified. The tread of the Association is
the tread of Christianity, and its tread means the crushing out of all elements which are not in harmony with Christian principles,—the crushing
out of caste and hatred. For who can oppress ? Who can tyrannize ;
when the stainless principles of the religion of Christ are living realities
in his heart? Who can dispute the rights of manhood when the soul is
illuminated by the light of the cross and the heart pulsates in harmony
with the meter of the Psalms ? As this organization advances much will
be done towards modifying Southern sentiment against the bronzed
American. A development into a higher civilization clothes men with
deeper thoughts as to the idea of religion, and things which were to them
intolerant, lose their intolerant features and the once disgutted parsonage
receives them with favor and libarality. The movement of the Association is playing an important part in the solution of the intricate problems
which address themselves to us. There is no human power, however
great, no human wisdom however searching, no inhumanities, however
torturous, that can stop the warm current of Christianity from bringing to
light the key to the solution of the Negro question. This is the domain
upon which is heard the significant tread of the Association It is also
warning the individual that is about to step upon the trap door of eternal loss, him whose head has grown white in sin, him whose ever-palpi-

tating heart causes him to detest his existence to put his trust in a never failing Providence. Here are two races each standing on tiptoe in breathless and painful anxiety endeavoring to decide as to the clouds or sunshine of the future, an advancing step and the murmerings as of distant waves are heard. It is not the tread of the ill drilled crusaders, nor is it the forces of Europe combined against Napoleon ; but it is a tread more destitute in its sweep than Euroclydon storms, more terrible than the heavings of the dyspeptic earth ; and yet more desirable than the morning dews of the Spring time. It is the tread of the Christian young men in the South.

It is the force whose sabres though unstrained and glittering in the sun will be the instruments in the annihilation of prejudice and the eventual happy solution of the Negro problem. For no people can live in perpetual hostility where the influences of the Christian religion are felt and growing. Much depends upon the young men in the settling of this race issue. And these are the ones that the Association is causing to be converted into the belief of the common brotherhood of man. This is admitted in that the malice existing in thebosoms of the old preponderates that which exists in the bosoms of the young. There are some associations that will permit colored representatives, which associations would not dared to have done it in the reconstruction period. And what the influence of the Association has done to modify sentiment in these States it will eventually do in modifying sentiment in all southern states.

The Arsociation is tearing down ignorance and endowing men with Christian education. It sparks lay hold on prejudice and it is forcing the confession of the brotherhood of man and the fatherhood of God.
True it is that the church is doing a great work along this line, but the work of the church does not reflect a single shadow upon the laudable endeavors of the Y. M. C. A. The Association treads upon territory where the church does not move. It secures the Christian membership of young men that never before attended church. It furnishes their rough hewn natures, enthrones good feeling and causes men to be regarded as men.

That the south is hostile towards us, cannot be denied. That the "Ox that treads the corn is muzzled," we admit; but when the tramp of God is heard, when the lights from Christian effort shall flash hither and thither, and the angelic strains of heavenly inspired music shall beat upon your ears the chains which bind prejudice to prejudice shall fall as silent as the dew and *all* men shall commune in loving fellowship. In conventions of the Associations men of both races come frequently in contact, and this frequency of contact tends to destroy what ill feeling that remains. It is not in the constitution of intelligent

humanity to permit an inordinate indulgence of antipathy towards each
other when they move on the same plane and labor in the same sphere.

When the dawning of Christianity shall effectually cover this southland—and we need not doubt that it will—bronzed Americans will not be
driven from their homes, ejected from first-class cars, nor massacred under the very eye of the law ; but men with unaffected sincerety will clasp
hands and pledge eternal friendship. This is the quarter towards which
the Association is moving, this is the part it is playing in the Christian
drama, and despite the distracted state of the country, despite the scaling
of cragged peaks and aspiring cliffs, despite its road of blood and death,
yet men will eventually, from where the gentle ripples kiss the floral
cheeks of the most distant south to where the echoes of the cruel lash
were most audible, be bereft of their barbaric inclinations, and rejoice
that men as men can meet, rejoice in the glorious march of the Y. M. C.
A , rejoice in its conquests, rejoice in its acquisitions for the kingdom of
God, and being touched by the inspiring chord of Christian enthusiasm,
shall burst forth in loud rejoicings, praising God for the institution of the
Association, praising im n that the Lamb can lie with the Lion, praising Him for its inestimable results to mankind, for the pacifying of awhole
nation, and for the saving of the isses of two centuries.

————o————

WHAT WE ARE DOING.

AN ADDRESS BY MR. E. D. W. JONES. DELIVERED AT THE RE-UNION OF
THE ALUMNI OF LIVINGSTONE COLLEGE MAY 28.

Mr President, Members of the Alumni, Ladies and Gentlemen :

In the history of universities and colleges, a custom has become prev-
alent among the students, to assemble around the pleasant haunts of their
Alma Mater, at a time designated by the association to report the results
of their labors, relate experiences, exchange ideas and catch renewed in-
spiration of college life. Thus with our own Livingstone, those who have
tasted of the sweets and bitters of life, seek a refuge from their daily
toils and gather around the festive board, relating their short experiences,
realized since they left the pleasant associations of college life.

Having set apart this the 28th day of May, 1890, to hold our meeting, we greet you with hearty welcome to the radient field, happy grove
and the beautiful structures, where once, you made your abode.

It is my purpose to give a short history of the Alumni Association,
and inform you of the work being done by some of its members. Start-
ing in the year 1887, it has met with unparaleld success, and all feel proud

of what has been accomplished in this broad field, where "the harvest is great but the laborers are few." Although among the latest, and a part of a young institution, she can boast of members, whose actions in the past bespeak for them glorious achievements in the future.

The first in the Classical Alumni is Rev. John A. D. Bloice A. B., Class '86, of St. Kitts, B. W. I. He attended the Boston Theological Institute, and there, among his more favored coadjutators, he honored the college from which he had received his education. He is now a minister stationed at Baltimore and giving to Zion such wide spread reputation, that under his pastorialship, another church has been added to the connection in that city. So Livingstone can boast of a grand representative who is promulgating the cause of God, and by his untiring labors is moulding a pure sentiment of public opinion that will some day give a sorrowing humanity of that place a possition for which they have long been craving.

Prof. J. D. Bibb A. B. of Montgomery, Ala., Class '87, is meeting with much success. In that far off southland where ignorance has moved unchecked, he is rapidly developing those powers of womanhood and manhood which are the elements of true excellence, and must tell in honor to him and his *Alma Mater*.

Rev. J. B. Colbert A B', Class '87, of Lancaster, S. C., is spreading the truths of Christianity in the far away State of Connecticut. They are proud of his efforts, and hope he will never tire in the work of marshalling his forces for God and humanity.

Prof. J. W, Colbert A. B., Class '87 Lancaster. S. C., is principal of a High school in Ga., and we are confident that progress will attend his work in that State. where such men are so much needed.

Prof. C. D. Howard A. B. Class '87, Tarboro, N, C.. is a teacher in the Winston Graded school, and being an intelligent Christian gentleman we feel assured that in his particular sphere his efforts will be rewarded with abundant success.

Mr. W. L. Henderson A. B., Class '87. Salisbury, N. C., has a splendid possition on the rail-road as postal clerk, from Washington to Charlotte. We can hope for success from his labors.

Prof. W. R. Douglass, Class '87, Lancaster, S. C., is holding the principalship of the High School at that place, and as an eye witness, we can speak of his work as progressing more and more, as each year some addition is made.

Rev. G. L. Blackwell A. B., Class '87, Statesville, N. C,, is holding the fort at Cambridgeport, Mass. He is a skilful manager, and his record stands out as substantial evidence to confirm all that has been said of his capabilities and willingness to utilize them for God and man.

Mrs. Esther Bingham, Class '87, Tarboro, N. C., being influenced by the Horace Greely sentiment, has gone West. She is an energetic woman and we are sure that she will be blessed with good results from her labors in the West.

Prof. I. D, Hargett A. B., Class '87, NewBerne, N. C., has not given much account of himself, but we hope he is doing well.

As my mind flashss over the work of '87, I am keenly reminded of the fact that all cannot be spoken of as mingling in the pursuits of this world but in the midst of life we are in death. Miss Ellen Dade is no more, but she leaves an example worthy of following by every woman of this Country. "Her soul is with the saints we trust".

Rev. R. H. Stitt, of Newburg, N. Y, Theological graduate of '87, is making for himself a wide spread reputation. He is one of the foremost colored men of N. Y., and performing the duty required of him, thereby adding to Livingstone praise and honor.

Rev. J. S. Caldwell, of Elizabeth City, N. C,, member of the same class, is doing well. May the condition of his people inspire him to press onward, never fall ng short of the mark,

Rev. W. B. Ferderson, of Beaufort. N. C., class of '89, is moving on, and we are sure that with such qualities that he possesses. His career will be one that none will be ashame to acknowledge.

As time will not permit us to speak of all seperately, those of the Normal Alumni must come under one head. This can be easily done, as most of them are engaged in teaching. Mrs. Maggie Colbert, Mrs. Clara V. Manly, Misses Anna Sloan, Gertie C. Hood, Addie McKnight, Minnie Sumner, Nora Tyler, Davis. Hannah Stewart, Nannie O'Kelly, Bettie Riddick, Mamie Lucas and Messrs J. H. McEntire, F. McNeil, Alonzo A. Rives, and Thomas J. Lomax, are all working in harmony with the sentiment taught at the College. Teaching the colored youths of the South is the work of well trained intelligence, and this has been the successful effort of Livingstone to prepare the students for work in whatever vocation in life they may choose to labor.

Now there are some of onr number who have long ago come to the realization that the school talked of arena is not strewn with flowers, but that is a hard place to be in, unless "soothed and sustained by an unfaltering trust" in God. We have three young ladies, and a young man that will soon leave us to battle with the adversities of life, and it is well for them to remember at the start that life is uncertain. Many are the times when the young men and women start out thoughtless of the great storm that will soon encounter if not sink to measureless depths, the frail barque that joyfully launched on life's apparently placid waters.

MENDELL V. JONES.

It is with a heart laden with sorrow that we put pen to paper, to say something of the death of our muchbeloved school-mate and associate on this paper, which occurred during the summer at Asheville, N. C.

Most of our readers are already aware of the sad event, but it is befitting that we should say something,—associated with him as we were.

His class-mates, his school-mates, his friends,- the readers of THE LIVING-STONE will miss him. The brain that created and the hand that indited the poetic effusions and other bits of literature, are hushed in death ; and the "Eagle" soars beyond the clouds, amid the ethereal regions where live the sainted. The fingered harp will be strung, the muse courted and the lute-like voice will sing to a grander, a more appreciative gathering than what this was on earth. And his reward shall be the crown of life, presented by the hand of Him who chaseth away all sorrow and giveth his beloved sleep.

We shall miss him ; and many will be the tears that shall course down the cheeks of those who knew and loved Mendell V. Jones.

We would say more, but the following from the pen of a white gentleman, of Massachusetts, expresses what we would say, so well, we gladly reproduce it here :

The above is the name of a boy who came into the High School of Worcester quite a number of years ago. He was of the race in whose behalf a long and wearisome war had been waged. He was exceedingly poor, and he has told me that he believed that his father was the man who, on dying at Tewksbury, furnished the material for the chief feature in the disgraceful investigation instigated by the, then, Governor Butler. It will seen, then, that he had little on his side to begin with ; save honesty and willingness. After a time in the school, he found it necessary to leave and to work, till he could command enough to begin again. On resuming, he remained with us till the middle of his Junior year when he went South. While in school he was noted for his readiness to work and for his ability in debate. At one time he was the president of his society, the Assembly. As I constantly supervised the working of these organizations, I had an opportunity to see how admirably he did his part. Every day that he went to the Worcester school, he had to do some manual labor. Self help and that constantly was the rule of his life.

Finally, he went to Salisbury, N. C., to enter Livingstone College under the dirrection of Dr. Price, and here in the holiday week of 1888, I called upon him. I found him happy and buoyant. He was pleased with his surroundings, and the President told me that he was pleased with the young man. He was fitting himself for the Christian ministry, with the expectations of carrying the blessed tidings to his own people in that long enslaved southland. Here, as in Worcester, he was working his way, and about a month ago he completed his Junior or third year and had before him only the final twelve months, and then was to come the fruitage time. During these years in the South he had acquired himself well. He was an associate editor of the college publication from the beginning, contributing to it many · excellent bits of verse, for he had the poetic impulse in a decided manner. When, in 1889, on Memorial Day, the loyal people of Salisbury and vicinity, gathered at the bural place of those who died in the foul Prison Pen, once hard by, to listen to the eloquent words of ex-Minister Langston, our friend Mendell was the poet of the occasion. He was fully equal to the opportunity, and many a day will pass ere those walls, enclosing our patriotic dead, will echo nobler strains than those uttered by our Massachusetts black boy. God bless him!

When the last college year was done he went away to the hills of western North Carolina to work at his trade of barbering in Asheville. During his southern residence, we had been in regular correspondence, and from th's new home he had already written me twice. From the last letter, I quote these words, referring to the grandeur of his surroundings, "Had I the time I could sit or walk the hours away in mute adoration of the hand work of God." He then refers to his earnings of the week, indicating his prospects for the coming year. This was written on June 8th, and just as I was thinking of answering, came the message that the young man was dead. Dead before he had begun his life work. Who can solve the plans of the Almighty? Here was a man who had devoted himself to the good of his people and the upbuilding of the kingdom of God; but he dies almost before he can lift a hand. He ceased to labor and to live, and has joined that throng of white robed ones who have put on immortality, and I can only disclose his merits here, hoping that others may emulate his virtues and industry and like him, find refuge in the hope of a blessed hereafter.—*Alfred S. Roe in the Worcester Methodist*

--------- o ---------

THE SITUATION.

READ ON DECORATION DAY BY W. F. FONVIELLE.

The civil strife is ended
By nearly thirty years,—
No more shall blood like rivers run,
Commingled with our tears.
No more shall North, East, South and West
In deadly conflict meet,—
No more shall Grant with others brave
The southern cause defeat.
No more the blood of millions
Shall fertile make the soil,—
No more the slave in bondage
Through winter's cold shall toil.
No more the buggle's ringing blast
Shall call the men to arms

At break of day or dead at night,
By signs of war's alarms.

The Prison Pens are all tourn down,
The prisoners are dead,
And thirteen thousand lie o'er there
With tomb-stones at their head.
With flowers, now, we decorate
The thirteen thousand graves,
For some of them belonged to Grant,
And some were Sherman's braves.
They fought like men for freedom's cause,
They perished, yea, they died,—
They're marshalled now in Death's brigade—
They were the nation's pride.

No Gettcysburg to read about,
With Picket's men in line—
No Wilderness nor great Bull Run,
Nor Petersburg's great Mine.
McDowell's men need not decamp;
There needs not for them too;
For all is o'er, the flag it waves
With stars, now forty-two,
So let us on this holiday
Rejoice and give our praise,
For these few tributes that we give
Will live in after days.

The Negro soldiers all fought well—
That's what Ben Butler said;
Though he stil lives, his Black brigade
Is numbered with the dead.
So after years of prayers and toil,
We meet here on this day
With flowers, music, speeches, and
Our yearly tribute pay.
We have not riches for to give,
In numbers we are weak;
And yet these tributes of respect
Will some day for us speak.
With men like Douglass, Langston Price,
Like Dancy, Fortune, Small,—
We only ask an equal chance;
We'll some day equal all.
With men like Grandison to speak,
We prove what we can do;
In riches many can surpass;
In eloquence they're few.

No more the cannon's deadly roar
Shall wake the soldiers tired,
The drums no more the rolls shall call,

Nor Sumpter's Fort be fired.
And some of you were soldiers too ;
But few of you remain ;
Where fifty men were mustered out
A hundred men were slain.
No longer foes, we hope, we trust
They never more shall be ;
But brothers in one common cause—
To lift humanity.

———o———

Editorial.

WELL, here we are again.

To day five o'clock, the College bell rings again, calling the wanderers home. And the eleventh session of our school has begun. We trust that it shall be so successful that God and man may both smile upon it approvingly.

STUDETS will please write us short letters outlining their work during the summer. We wish to publish them for the benefit of our friends —colored and wh te, who are anxious to know what you are doing both north and south alike.

THOSE who are indebted to the LIVING-STONE will please forward the amount due us. Others would do well to subscribe. The price is 50 cents per year.

THOSE who failed to receive their paper this summer need not be surprised. As a rule college publications are not issued during the vacation. We issue during the college year. We only tried it last summer as an experiment.

THE LIVING-STONE is purely literary, and will at all times be devoted to the best interest of the students, the alumni and Livingstone College. It will not be our purpose to dabble in politics, either one way or the other; so no one need have any fear of subscribing. Our object is not to make money, but to make the paper self sustaining; and to this end we ask those who are in arrears to please remit what they owe us.

THE subscription list of the LIVING-STONE is not prescribed by any certain lines. We have subscribers north, east, south and west and some of them represent the brain and capital of the country of both races. It lives for all.

IF you are thinking of going to school, send for a catalogue, which will give you all of the desired information concerning our school. Address Dr. J. C. Price or Prof E. Moore.

THE editor being absent, the Managing editor has done all the work on this issue—writing, type setting, printing, binding and mailing.

MOST of the students have worked hard, the past summer, in order that they might make money enough to tide them over during the present session. God grant that they have been successful.

MR. Geo. H. Wilkerson, (Pat,) class '93 will be the next editor of this paper. The responsibility falls upon a bright young man. He w e ds a facile pen and has a dash of the critic in his make-up ; and like the rest of us, he knows the art preservative. There is no doubt but what he will edit it with as much credit to himself and the College as did Mr. Johnson his successor.   Here is our ☞, Pat, we welcome you.

LIVINGSTONE College is in possession of possibly the first portrait of President Lincoln in existence. It is a painting by the great artist, Cobb,—the value of which is $1000. It was presented to the College on commencement day of last session by our staunch friend, Mr. Chas. G. Chase of Boston, Mass., through Editor Jno. C. Dancy. Besides this the College has an excellent likeness of David Livingstone, the great African explorer, a picture of the great anti-slavery agitator, William Lloyd Garrison, a handsome picture of the rail-road magnet, G. P. Huntington, and still another of Bishop J. W. Hood D. D. This is our picture gallery in embryo ; which will some day burst forth in resplendent beauty.

———o———

THE ALUMNI.

Miss M. I. Hood, Normal '99 has been spending the summer at Wilmington, N. C.

The reliable A. A. Rives still holds down a case in the "Star of Zion" office during the day ; and at night serenades somebody over the way on his guitar to the strain of "Little Bunch of Lilacs." That's Lonnie.

Mr. Frank McNeil, Normal '88 has been conducting a large school at Harrison, N. C.

Rev. Jno. A. D. Bloice, '86, the popular young pastor of the A. M. E. Zion church at Baltimore, Md , has gone on a three months trip to England.

Our former editor, Mr. B. A. Johnson, '90 has been offered and has accepted a position, as assistant principal in a high school of Birmingam, Ala.

Mr E. V. Davis Normal '87 has gone to Baltimore to read law.

Rev. W. B. Fenderson '89, who is at present a student in the Gammon Theological school of Atlanta, Ga., is visiting friends in this state.

School - Students Here and There.

The eleventh session of Livingstone College begins Oct., 1st and the outlook is that it will be even more prosperous than what last session was.

Miss Dora L. Cox has been teaching at Mangum, N. C., and visiting friends at Rockingham, Charlotte, and Concord.

Our pedestrian, W. U. Davenport, has carried his linen duster and white derby down in Pamplico, where he is teaching the young ideas how to shoot, fighting mosquitoes, and making himself humorous with the sand flies. By-the-way, Will was assistant secretary of the Eastern Carolina Fair Association, which was held in NewBerne the latter part of August.

Mr. Samuel A. Kelsey spent some time in Asheville this summer, but he is back and can be found at the same old stand—sticking type for the "Star of Zion."

Miss Gertie S. G. Holmes who has been conducting a large school at Pineville has returned and is now ready to enter school.

Our sympathy goes out to Miss Lula E. Love in-her bereavement over the death of her beloved mother, which sad event occured at her home in Asheville some time ago.

Dr. Price has been lecturing in Kansas, Nebraska and Minnesotta; Prof. Moore has been conducting a teachers institute at Greensboro; Prof Goler has been actively engaged in church work at Winston; Profs. Atkins and Suggs have been traveling in the interest of the College; Miss Richardson is off on a triy to Charlotte; Miss Gould spent her vacation here and Miss Hood has been summering a few days in Asheville.

Miss Martha A. Wilkins is teaching in Nash county and is having success.

That High School at Plymouth, N. C., which J. W. McDonald went to take charge of, proved to be a big affair under his principalship. The students numbered up in the hundreds, and "Mac" seems to have struck it rich.

Our smiling friend, H. Wilder, is teaching in Wilson county, where he is justly popular and succeeds in getting the same school every summer.

The placid Miss Jennie W. Green is teaching in the mountains and seems to enjoy it immensely.

Prof. R. B. McCrary principal of the Reidsville Graded school, will fill the chair in Livingstone College, made vacant by Prof. Atkins who has accepted the principalship of the Winston Graded school.

Mrs. Jackson, our Matron, and daughter Miss Alexandria, have spent part of their vacation very pleasantly at Wilmington and the seashore.

Miss P. A. Moore has spent the summer pleasantly in Asheville.

Our student merchants, Messrs Richardson and Ardis seem to be satisfied. Mr. Richardson has been over home for a few days vis't'ng relatives, while the religious-inclined Mr. Ardis has been conducting a revival a few miles out in the country; and several new members have been added to the church list.

Miss Ada Battle, who won the medal in the Freshman contest for the best composition by a young lady, is teaching in Wilson county.

The Managing editor has been pretty much over the state the past summer and found most of the students hard at work, and anxious to return to school.

We met that eccentric personage, A. F. Moore in Goldsboro some time ago, and in company with him boarded the cars for NewBerne. He declared his intention of winning a premium at the NewBerne Fair, and return to school this session.

Mr. A. A. Crooke has been spending the summer in Brooklyn, N. Y., and preaches accasionally in the churches of that city. His sermons are spoken of very highly.

Miss Annie E. Hill is teaching in Wayne county. She has a well disciplined school of 86 scholars.

Rev. R. A. Morrisey, who won the gold medal for oratory in the last Junior contest, was here a few days ago. As a Rev he bids fair to equal that wonderful six of Livingstone College, Revs. Jno. A. D. Bloice, C. L. Blackwell, J. B Colbert, R. H. Stitt, J. S. Caldwell, and W. B Fenderson. Educated, refined, bright—every one of them. They all are cash subscribers of the LIVING-STONE. We love them all; and may God bless them in their efforts to raise fallen humanity.

---o---

LIVINGSTONE MARRIAGE BELLS.

Miss Lillian Fleming of Morganton, N. C., to Rev. G. S. Adams a former student of Livingstone College.

On Friday Sept, 5th Miss Jennie E. Harris of Concord, class of '87 was married to Dr. J. T. Williams of Charlotte. The LIVING-STONE tenders congratulations, and hopes thattheir sail upon the matrimonial sea may be a pleasure trip unmarred by storms.

Cards were out last month announcing the marriage of Miss Viola Lovett of Montgomery, Ala., to Mr. J. D. Bibb, class '87, which happy event took place on the 18th at Clinton Chapel in that city. Our congratulations. May there be plenty of orange blossoms, but no thorns.

Things of the Hour.

THINGS CRITICISED AND COMMENTED UPON.

The spring came ; and nature budded, blossomed, and bloomed. The three summer months helped to mature and clothe it in richest green And now autumn has put forth its fiery fingers and touched nature's hand- i-work, and the trees have doned their crimson gowns.   The frosts of October and November will pluck the trimmings from the grand old monarchs of the forest, and the winter months will clothe them in unblem- ished whiteness.

* *
*

Recollections of General Grant is the name of a little volume, neatly bound, bearing the autograph of Geo. W. Childs.   It is a gem within it self, and relates many pleasing incidents in the life of the lamented Gen. eral.   It is the latest literary effort of this great writer and philanthropist. The names of the author and subject are enough to insure it a great sale. It is published by Lipp'ncott & Co., of Philadelphia, neatly bound in col- ored cloth with gilt top, rough edges, price $1.00.

* *
*

The Negro convention which convened in Raleigh during the month of August, asked for an Agricultural and Mechanical College, similar to that which the state has errected and is opperating for the whites. Should they see fit to establish such a school for the Negros of the state, ac- cording to the provisions of the Morrill bill, each school would receive $12.500 a year   Let us hope that it will be established.

* *
*

The "State Chronicle" is authority for the statement, that Prof. E. A. Johnson Principal of the Washington Graded School of Raleigh, N. C., has prepared and will soon issue a history or text book of the Negro race, for use in the schools.   The book will treat of the Negro race from its or- igin to date, giving a history of the race at home, in slavery, the exodus movement to Liberia, its work and progress, and all facts in connection with the race, This is something the race has been sadly in need of for a long time. We study the histories of our country and states, but no truthful account of the Negro is given in any of these ; and in some of the historical text books he is altogether forgotten.   This will be the first and only book of its kind in existence.   Certainly Col. Geo. Williams has written a very excellent history of the Negro race, but it is too voluminous far anything like school purposes.

—— —— o—— ——

MONEY MAKING IN VACATION TIME.

About one year ago I procured instructions. for plating with Gold

Silver and Nickle; and devoted my summer vacation to plating. In 43 days I cleared $391.10, a sufficient amount to pay my expenses for the college year. At nearly every house I plated spoons, castors, or jewelery and find it pleasant, instructive and profitable. My brother in 19 days cleared $162.40. Knowing that there are many desiring an education who have not the necessary means, I trust that my experience will be to such, a joyful revelation. By sending 25 cents to The Zanesville Chemical Co., Zanesville, Ohio, you will receive dirrections for making Gold, Silver and Nickle solutions, with the necessary instructions for using them, and in an hours practice you will be quite proficient.   NELLIE B. —

Streggle's Column.

The same rules that governed the palace in Dodge Hall last session hold good this session. For fear somebody has forgotten them, and to impress them more fully upon your mind, I have the consent of the editors to publish them in this issue of the LIVING-STONE.

They are as follows:

Wipe your feet at the door, and be sure and let somebody know you are coming in.

Don't sit on the bed. Chairs are made to sit on, and there are two in the room.

Don't open the piano without permission, its a little out of fix, but if you are anxious to play, make it known by signs if you can't talk.

Don't throw your hat on the bed, you'll find a hat-rack on the wall.

Don't sit on the trunks; they cost money now-a-days.

Don't borrow my umbrella without letting me know you have it, you might forget to return it, and then I'd have to borrow one without letting anybody know anything about it.

Please don't forget and set on the hot stove, you might rub the polish off.

Don't drag your feet on the Brussell's carpet, they have stopped giving them away.

Please don't ask me to let your cook sweet potatoes to punch over on the stove unless you promise to divide.

Don't ask me about the weather. I don't belong to the Weather Bureau, and can't tell about it at all.

Don't ask me to loan you money in the first place, I haven't any, in the second place it's bad policy, an attack on the enterprising class.

With love and due to students idol and so on, I am yours, A.